Brain

MW01520424

All the best puzzles, games, and fun from the pages of CREATIVE KIDS magazine!

ISBN # 1-882664-13-2

Cover artwork by Rikki Conley

Table of Contents

Introduction

I don't really know whose idea this book was, but it was a great idea. Growing up, I had a subscription to a children's magazine, and I looked forward to receiving it each month. When I got it, the first thing I did was find the games and work them. My guess is that many of you do the same. Games take our minds off other things. Once when I was in the hospital, a visitor brought me a book of puzzles. Hours seemed to pass much faster when I set my mind to solving puzzles and mastering the games in that book. So, I present to you this book.

My hope is that none of you have to while away hours in a hospital, but that maybe on a rainy day, or when it's too hot or cold to go outside and play, you will pull out this book and find hours of enjoyment.

The editorial staff at *Creative Kids* has spent months finding the very best puzzles and games from old issues of the magazine. Special thanks to Kellie Maxwell for the countless hours she spent digging through old mail and magazines to find puzzles.

On the pages that follow, you will find logic puzzles, mazes, board games, crossword puzzles, word games, riddles, and much, much more.

I must thank a few people who made this book possible. First, thanks to Fay Gold, who served as editor of *Creative Kids* for 11 years and first hooked many of you on the clever games and puzzles found in the magazine. I must also thank Stephanie Stout for giving the magazine new direction and teaching me the fundamentals of being an editor. Thanks for passing down to me such an outstanding magazine.

Finally, and most importantly, thanks to all of you who are the reason there is a *Creative Kids* magazine. These games were written and designed by you. They are yours. Enjoy them and have fun!

Andrea Harrington

Solar System Word Search

Find the words from the word list in this puzzle.
Words may be up, down, across, and backwards.

```
A N K P S U V A E B R L M Z C
X O B K L R J L V D O P O G F
S N T A Z A Y K C O F L O M H
T L A U V N P O L S N R N B W
A A K B P U E Z U W Z Q C L M
R C P A U S S A T U R N D P Z
L D M E R C U R Y Z O E P A P
P I F S O L A R H I K P Z B L
U H S N P Z H Z W J X T D F U
K N A P T A B L V U N U O C T
X Z T E L E S C O P E N Z H O
C Y E A J I X O P I R E L N K
R B L R Z A G M G T X I V O Z
A O L T S R N E L E W C N P K
T W I H I X S T W R G H L G E
E O T M W S U N S P O T E A S
R D E W F C L S Q K H R U E B
S U N E V G V W L R T S B H L
M E Z M A R S B O T U M J I S
B L A C K H O L E N O A Z L T
```

Black hole
Comet
Crater
Earth
Jupiter
Mars
Mercury
Moon
Neptune
Nova
Orbit
Pluto
Rings
Satellite
Saturn
Solar
Star
Sun spot
Telescope
Uranus
Venus

Puzzle by
**Scott Robinson
Edison, NJ**

Spacey Crossword

Using the clues below, fill in the blanks of the puzzle on the next page.

Across:

2. What this crossword puzzle is about
5. Planet farthest from the sun
6. The planet named after the sea god
9. The red planet
11. The Milky Way and Andromeda are _____
12. Halley's _____
14. The pinpoints of light in the night sky
15. The planet closest to the sun
17. The planet on its side

Down:

1. A Russian astronaut
3. What "Voyager" missions were sent out to do
4. A ringed planet
7. Our planet
8. E.T. was one of these
10. A "deadly nothing"
13. An American space traveller is an _____
16. A _____ blasts people into space

Puzzle by
**Colin Pridy
British Columbia,
Canada**

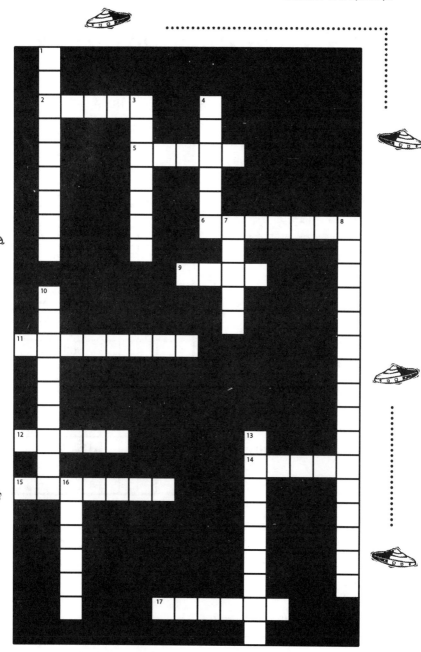

Astronauts Landing

Jason Jenkins, Altoona, AL

Using the clues and the grid provided, solve the puzzle.

1. John Glenn did not fly Freedom 7, and he couldn't have anyway because he was sick in the hospital on May 5, 1961.
2. Tereshkova and Gagarin are the Soviet cosmonauts who flew the Vostok Crafts.
3. Alan Shepard was not the first American to orbit, and he did not fly the Apollo or the Friendship.
4. Gagarin, the bearded cosmonaut, did not see the Vostok 6, which did not fly in 1961.
5. Vostok 1 was not the first on the moon and did not move off the pad during a month ending in "y."
6. Freedom 7 never made it to the moon and did not operate in June, July, or February.
7. Neil Armstrong was not the first American in orbit, and he was not selected to fly the Friendship.
8. The first woman in space did not go in a winter month or a month ending with "y."
9. A Russian was the first in space.
10. The pilot who flew the Apollo 11 did not go in 1962.
11. Alan was the first American in space.

	Glenn	Tereshkova	Armstrong	Shepard	Gagarin	
						April 1961
						May 1961
						July 1969
						June 1963
						February 1962
						Vostok 1
						Freedom 7
						Apollo 11
						Vostok 6
						Friendship 7
						1st in space
						1st on moon
						1st Am. in space
						1st woman astronaut
						1st Am. in orbit

Outer Space Crossword

Matthew Bugaj, Chittenango, NY

Across:

4. The center of our solar system
5. A planet with visible rings
6. The shape of our solar system
7. The planet named after the Roman goddess of love
11. The planet named after the Roman god of the sea
14. A group of planets, stars, comets, asteroids, and meteors
15. The planet that we live on
16. A meteor that has hit Earth's surface

Down:

1. The group of asteroids between Mars and Jupiter
2. The red planet
3. The planet with a huge red spot
8. The seventh planet from the sun
9. The planet named after the Roman messenger of the gods
10. What you might see one of in the night sky
12. A comet that broke into Earth's atmosphere
13. The planet farthest from the sun

Confused Cats

Three girls each own a cat. There was a mix-up, and the cats went home with the wrong girls. Match each girl with her last name, her cat's name, and the color of the cat.

1. The orange cat is not named Pumpkin.
2. Pumpkin went to the Brown's house.
3. Sue's cat is gray.
4. Ann's black cat went to the Smith's.
5. Skittles was supposed to go to the Brown's house.

6. Sally's neighbors are the Browns.
7. Skittles belongs to Ann.
8. Sally went to the Silver's house to look for Dopey.

	Brown	Silver	Smith	Pumpkin	Skittles	Dopey	Orange	Gray	Black
Sally									
Ann									
Sue									

Puzzle by
Jenny Giddens
Udall, KS

Picture Graph

Leslie Chiaventone, Herrin, IL

Plot the following list of ordered pairs. The first number is the horizontal number on the graph, and the second number is the vertical number. Connect the dots along the way until you come to the word STOP, then lift your pencil. Begin with the next group of numbers and connect them as you go. Complete column one before moving to column two, and so on.

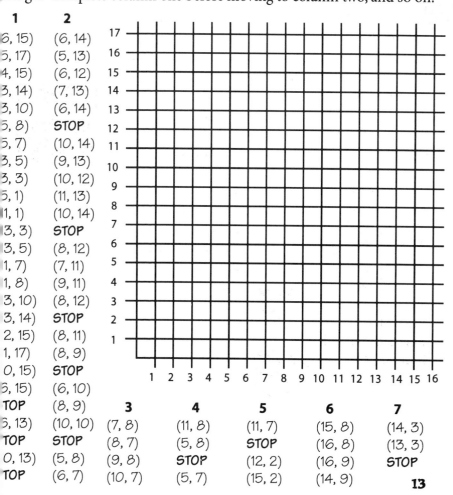

1	2	3	4	5	6	7
(6, 15)	(6, 14)					
(5, 17)	(5, 13)					
(4, 15)	(6, 12)					
(3, 14)	(7, 13)					
(3, 10)	(6, 14)					
(5, 8)	STOP					
(5, 7)	(10, 14)					
(3, 5)	(9, 13)					
(3, 3)	(10, 12)					
(5, 1)	(11, 13)					
(1, 1)	(10, 14)					
(3, 3)	STOP					
(3, 5)	(8, 12)					
(1, 7)	(7, 11)					
(1, 8)	(9, 11)					
(3, 10)	(8, 12)					
(3, 14)	STOP					
(2, 15)	(8, 11)					
(1, 17)	(8, 9)					
(0, 15)	STOP					
(6, 15)	(6, 10)					
STOP	(8, 9)	(7, 8)	(11, 8)	(11, 7)	(15, 8)	(14, 3)
(5, 13)	(10, 10)	(8, 7)	(5, 8)	STOP	(16, 8)	(13, 3)
STOP	STOP	(9, 8)	STOP	(12, 2)	(16, 9)	STOP
(0, 13)	(5, 8)	(10, 7)	(5, 7)	(15, 2)	(14, 9)	
STOP	(6, 7)					**13**

Hobbies Word Scramble

Unscramble the following words. Each word will be the name of a hobby.

1. itgnapni   _ _ _ _ _ _ _ _
2. gacidnn   _ _ _ _ _ _ _
3. oskabechr igridn _ _ _ _ _ _ _ _ _ _ _ _ _ _ _
4. oapni   _ _ _ _ _
5. tosrps   _ _ _ _ _ _
6. imscu   _ _ _ _ _
7. eelginaedhcr   _ _ _ _ _ _ _ _ _ _ _ _
8. hinfgis   _ _ _ _ _ _
9. pagimcn   _ _ _ _ _ _ _
10. arketa   _ _ _ _ _ _
11. mwgisinm   _ _ _ _ _ _ _ _
12. wgrdani   _ _ _ _ _ _ _
13. algeldornirlb   _ _ _ _ _ _ _ _ _ _ _ _
14. eic gnastik   _ _ _ _ _ _ _ _ _ _
15. igknsi   _ _ _ _ _ _

Puzzle by
Lorna Borchardt
Lometa, TX

Scrambled Phrases

Unscramble the following phrases to find clichés.

1. srtut em
2. okol refebo oyu apel
3. a nyenp evdas si a nnpey eadern
4. het rylea idrb tseg eth mwor
5. on ianp, on iang
6. ese a enynp, cikp ti pu nda lla eht ayd uoy illw vaeh odog ukcl
7. hnew ti anisr ti orusp
8. ilrAp owsrshe ignbr ayM owresfl
9. ti si wysaal rksadet frbeeo het wnda

Scramble by
Laurie Miller
Ft. Smith, AR

1. ksantig no nhti cie
2. ndot nocut ryuo cchkiesn feobre yteh tchah
3. rehwe htrese a lilw srthee a ywa
4. na plpea a ayd ekeps hte netsidt waay
5. htignigf keli stac nda dsgo
6. oot anmy kcoos iopls eht torbh
7. fede a dlco, vetsra a verfe

Scramble by
Jason Taylor
Stratford, MO

Lunch at School

Danielle Dunn, Sugar Land, TX

During lunch, Kathy and her four friends sat together at their usual table and discussed their favorite subjects. Each was willing to listen to the others, but was most eager to tell about her own favorite class. Each girl had a different drink, and no two girls had the same favorite subject. Using the clues and diagram below, determine where each girl sat, what her favorite subject was, and what drink she had that day.

1. The two girls on the west side of the table have sodas (with different brand names), while those on the east side have more nutritious drinks.
2. Kathy and Danielle are seated next to each other on the east side of the table.
3. The two girls who like science and math are seated on the west side of the table.
4. Rachel is in seat 5. The girl whose favorite subject is English is seated next to Rachel.
5. The girl who especially enjoys health class is drinking milk.
6. Danielle does not like health class. She does, however, drink orange juice every day at lunch.
7. Rachel loves history class. Kim loves science.
8. Jessica is drinking a Dr Pepper. Kim is in seat 2.
9. The girls' drinks are Dr Pepper, Diet Coke, apple juice, milk, and orange juice.

1
2
3
4
5

Lunch Bunch

Sophia Wang, Bowling Green, KY

Use the clues below to figure out what each person had for his or her main meal, drink, and dessert.

1. Joe doesn't eat or drink anything that comes from animals and does not eat dessert or drink carbonated drinks.
2. Hank made everyone laugh when he ordered a breakfast food and soda.
3. Elizabeth did not get beef or Coke.
4. The boy who got pizza and Coke likes Mary.
5. Mr. Lowe scolded Mary for spilling pickles and ketchup on her blouse.
6. Elizabeth refused to eat any cold or frozen desserts.
7. Mary, who didn't order soda, was glad that she ordered a milkshake.
8. The man who ordered Pepsi and ice cream talked to the boy who ordered Coke and a blizzard.
9. Mr. Lowe asked for medium rare and steak sauce.

	Hank	Mary	Mr. Lowe	Joe	Elizabeth	Andy	
Hamburger							Main Meal
Steak							
Salad							
Eggs							
Pizza							
Chicken							
Coke							Drink
Soda							
Milk							
Orange Pop							
Water							
Pepsi							
Ice Cream							Dessert
Candy Bar							
Banana Split							
Blizzard							
Milk Shake							
None							

Desk Arrangements

Place each student in his or her correct desk.

1. Tom sits two desks left of George.
2. Sharon sits next to Jodi.
3. Jodi sits two desks away from John.
4. John sits two desks in back of Nick.
5. Nick sits next to George.
6. Cindy sits two desks in front of Mike.
7. John always turns his head right and talks to Jill.
8. Jason is very bad and has to sit very close to the teacher.
9. Cary leaves the room a lot to go to the bathroom, so she sits next to the door.
10. Tom throws notes to Jason, and Doug tries to reach up and grab them.
11. Michele sits on the back row.
12. George pulls on Judy's hair.
13. Melissa doesn't like being the only girl in the middle row.
14. The fourth row is empty.
15. Nathan copies off of Cindy's paper.
16. The teacher yells at Neil to keep his stuff off the heater.
17. In math they pass their papers to the left, and Mitch corrects Cary's paper.
18. Neil throws spit balls at Judy, but Julie catches them and throws them back.
19. Sharon sits two desks behind Tom.
20. Doug sits next to Jane.

Teacher's Desk

Door

Puzzle by
John Jackson
Nick Petges
Batavia, IL

18

Can You Find Your Way?

Trace over this picture without lifting your pencil or tracing over any line. You may start anywhere on the picture.

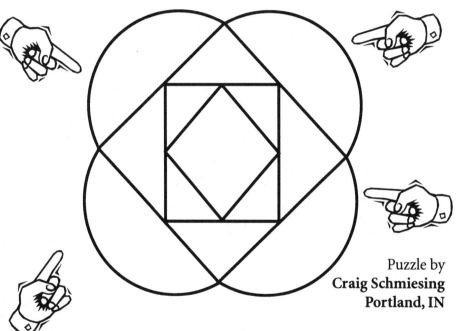

Puzzle by
Craig Schmiesing
Portland, IN

The Lady's Fate
There once was a lady from Greb,
Who got caught in a big spider's web.
Her husband, a coward,
Just watched her devoured,
By a big, hairy spider named Ebb.

Limerick by
Scott Trobaugh
Bridgewater, VA

19

The Shopping Spree

Six boys bought items in their favorite colors. Using the clues, figure out which boy bought what item and in what color.

	Hat	Socks	Sneakers	Pants	Shirt	Jacket	Brown	Blue	Green	Red	Black	Yellow
Kevin												
George												
Mike												
Harry												
Chadd												
Chris												

1. Kevin does not like red, yellow, blue, or brown.
2. Mike bought a hat.
3. George bought something blue.
4. Harry didn't purchase socks, a jacket, or pants.
5. Kevin did not buy socks, sneakers, or pants.
6. Chadd later borrowed Kevin's black item to wear with his green jacket.
7. The boys are: the one who purchased brown socks, George, the one who bought red sneakers, the boy who got the yellow hat, Chadd, and Kevin.

Puzzle by
Emily Brown
Hudson, NH

Fruit and Vegetable Stand Mix-Up

Jane and Mark are setting up a fruit and vegetable stand. Use these clues to help them set up their stand.

1. The carrots are before the apples.
2. The green beans are third.
3. The apples are before the green beans.
4. The pecans are between the broccoli and tomatoes.
5. The cauliflower is last.
6. The tomatoes are ninth.
7. The peaches are right after the green beans.
8. The peas are between the pears and the peaches.

Puzzle by
**Eryn Hardy and
Lorna Borchardt
Lometa, TX**

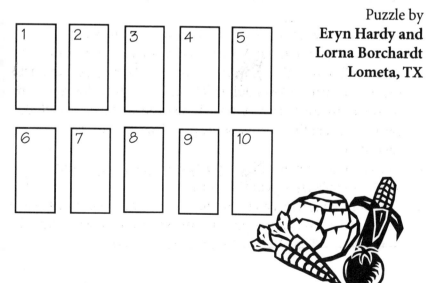

1	2	3	4	5

6	7	8	9	10

Shop 'Til You Drop

Kim Haddix and Sarah Hensley, Cincinnati, OH

Players: 2-4
Object: To get the most points
Directions:

1. Choose a color for each player's starting point.
2. Roll a die to see who goes first, second, etc., beginning with the highest number.
3. Only roll the die once for each turn.
4. The first player rolls the die. Move however many blocks you roll.
5. If you land on a space that has a store's name on it, move to that store. If the space is black, then move to the store of your choice. If another player gets to a store before you, you must keep rolling at each of your turns until you reach an available store.
6. Once you move into a store, pick a card from that store.(The cards are found in the appendix on page 87.) Read the card out loud to all of the other players. The score keeper writes whether the player earns or loses points. The card says whether you earn or lose from one to three points. When you are finished with the card, place it at the bottom of the pile. There are six cards for each store.
7. The game continues with people searching for empty stores and/or people taking cards in turn.
8. The game ends when all six of the cards for any one store have been used up. When the game is over, the scorekeeper counts all of the points. The player with the most points wins.

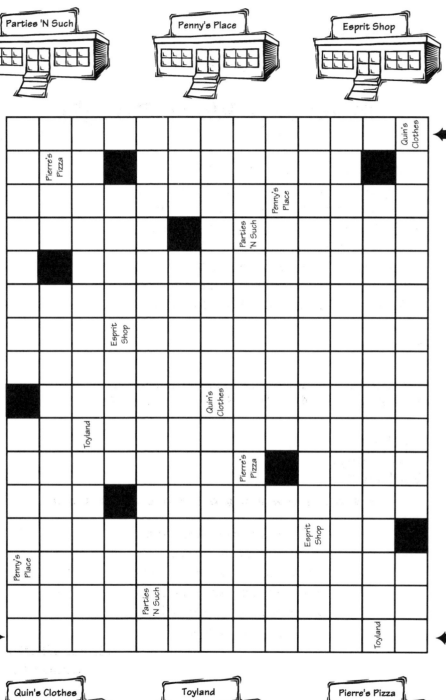

Parties 'N Such

Penny's Place

Esprit Shop

Quin's Clothes

Pierre's Pizza

Penny's Place

Parties 'N Such

Esprit Shop

Quin's Clothes

Pierre's Pizza

Toyland

Penny's Place

Parties 'N Such

Esprit Shop

Toyland

Quin's Clothes

Toyland

Pierre's Pizza

Mystery Word Puzzle

1. My first letter is in tea, but not in the.
2. My next two letters are in call, but not in can.
3. My eighth letter is in tour but, not in rut.
4. My fifth letter is in frog, but not in from.
5. My last letter is in row, but not in won.
6. My seventh letter is in toward, but not in coward.
7. My fourth letter is in zip, but not in zap.
8. My sixth letter is in ate, but not in eight.

What am I?

— — — — — — — — —
1　2　3　4　5　6　7　8　9

Puzzle by
Jeremy Grogg
Portland, IN

● ● ● ● ● ● ● ● ● ● ● ● ● ● ● ● ● ● ● ●

Old Mother Twitchett
has but one eye
and a long tail which she can let fly
And every time she goes over a gap
she leaves a bit of her tail in a trap.
What is she?

Melissa Wheeler
Medford, OR

Jumble

Unscramble the five words below. Using the circled letters, form an answer to the question.

AMSE

YIOLGOB

ERCAIMA

TASETL

LOCFIFAI

What animal followed Mary to school?

Puzzle by
Lisa Vannice
Phoenix, AZ

=

+ Magnificent ‑
Mathematicians

X
Nick Mayo, Boaz, AL ÷

These people were great mathematicians. Each originated from a different country and had different breakthroughs. Use the clues to help find out who came from where and what his breakthrough was.

1. Regiomontanus and Euclid were from nations starting with "G."
2. The British genius did not create trigonometry and did not devise his new idea in 1614.
3. John Napier's neighborhood is located in a land with a "c" in its spelling.
4. The Greek did not conceive trigonometry or calculus.
5. The inventor who would wear a kilt invented logarithms.
6. The oldest man enjoyed working with planes and angles.
7. The mathematician from Britain originated his invention in the 17th century.
8. Euclid was not from Germany, and he was not alive in the 16th century.
9. Regiomontanus was older than John Napier.

	Greece	Germany	Britain	Scotland	300 B.C.	1614	1687	1533	Geometry	Calculus	Trigonometry	Logarithms
Regiomontanus												
John Napier												
Euclid												
Sir Isaac Newton												

Five in a Row

Players: 2 to 6
Directions:
1. Roll a die. The player with the highest number will start.
2. The object of the game is to get five of the same numbers in a vertical or horizontal row.
3. When you roll the die and get 1, 2, 3, or 4, you put the number you got in one box.
4. When you roll the die and get 5 or 6, you can put the number in two boxes of your choice.
5. Materials are one die, a pencil, and the game board.

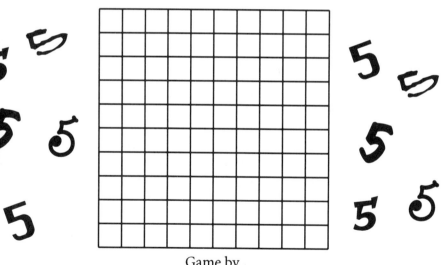

Game by
David Charpentier
West Allis, WI

Picture Graph

Kristin Pankey, Herrin, IL

Plot the following list of ordered pairs. The first number is the horizontal number on the graph, and the second number is the vertical number. Connect the dots along the way until you come to the word STOP, then lift your pencil. Begin with the next group of numbers and connect them as you go. Complete column one before moving to column two, and so on.

1	2	3	4	5
(3, 18)	(4, 15)	(7, 9)	(12, 12)	STOP
(4, 16)	STOP	(9, 10)	STOP	
(2, 17)		(9, 12)		(9, 4)
(3, 18)	(4, 15)	(8, 15)	(9, 11)	(9, 2)
STOP	(2, 13)	STOP	(12, 12)	STOP
	(3, 11)		STOP	
(4, 16)	(3, 8)	(11, 16)		(8, 3)
(4, 15)	(4, 5)	(11, 13)	(9, 12)	(10, 3)
(6, 15)	(6, 5)	(12, 12)	(11, 13)	STOP
(6, 16)	(6, 7)	(12, 10)	(12, 14)	
(4, 16)	STOP	(10, 8)	(13, 14)	(11, 4)
STOP		(8, 8)	(11, 13)	(11, 2)
	(4, 16)	(6, 7)	STOP	STOP
(6, 15)	(4, 19)	STOP		
(7, 11)	STOP		(7, 4)	(12, 2)
(7, 9)		(6, 6)	(5, 4)	(12, 3)
(6, 7)	(6, 16)	(7, 6)	(5, 3)	(11, 3)
(5, 8)	(7, 19)	(9, 7)	(7, 3)	STOP
(5, 11)	STOP	(13, 7)	(7, 1)	
(4, 13)		(13, 9)	(5, 1)	

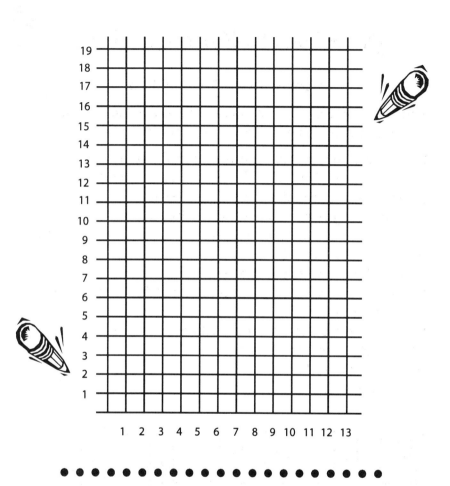

Riddle Time

What is first burnt, then beaten, then stepped on by animals with long faces?

Stacie Roth, Portland, IN

A Mixed-Up Car Race

Matthew Parker, Fort Smith, AR

Seven boys were in a car race. Use the clues to figure out who drove what car, and in what order they crossed the finish line.

1. Bill came in right after the person in the orange car.
2. Rob came in right after the person in the green car.
3. Matt barely beat the person in the red car.
4. Zack barely beat the person in the blue car.
5. Chad does not like the colors red, yellow, white, orange, and black.
6. Adam's favorite color is blue.
7. Matt's favorite two colors are white and black.
8. Rob and Peter like orange and black, but Rob likes orange better than black.
9. Bill came in second to last and barely beat the black car.
10. The yellow car came in sixth.
11. Matt's car is the fastest.
12. The green car came in fourth.

	Red	Blue	Yellow	White	Orange	Green	Black	1st	2nd	3rd	4th	5th	6th	7th
Bill														
Rob														
Zack														
Adam														
Chad														
Peter														
Matt														

Horse Race

Kelly Hackathorn, Ashtabula, OH

Four horse owners hired jockeys to race their horses. Use the clues to figure out each horse's name, which jockey rode each horse, and in which order they crossed the finish line.

1. Becky rode the horse that won first place.
2. Kate's horse, Magic, placed higher than the horse ridden by Emily, but lower than Eclipse.
3. Lightning and Princess (in no particular order) were the last two horses to cross the finish line.
4. Jim's jockey, Laura, won him one place lower than Ceri.
5. Emily and Princess won third place.

	Magic	Lightning	Princess	Eclipse	Laura	Jennie	Becky	Emily	1st place	2nd place	3rd place	4th place
Kate												
Jim												
Jessie												
Ceri												

French Explorers

1. Louis discovered a river. He was not the youngest.
2. The man who investigated Canada did not explore in an odd year.
3. Jacques discovered a river. The year was before the three other explorers discovered anything.
4. The man who explored Canada did not have an "e" in the second wor of his last name.
5. The man who found the Gulf of Mexico had an eight in the year of h discovery. He did not make his discovery in the early 17th century.
6. The 1534 explorer had only one "a" in his last name. He did not sear for the river partially located in the south.
7. Robert had two parts in his last name. He did not discover the lanc mentioned in this puzzle.

	Joliet	de Champlain	Cartier	La Salle	Gulf of Mexico	Mississippi River	Canada	St. Lawrence	1682	1673	1534	1608
Samuel												
Robert												
Jacques												
Louis												

Puzzle by
Meredith Licht
Gadsden, AL

Early Revolutionary Days

Kelli Miller, Atchison, KS

```
L I N C M M I D N I G H T T T I O N L D
B I T H C I H I D N I T O M A O N D Y A
N N O T G N I X E L L I O M N X E L I N
I X E L B U N K C E R T S R R S U R E N
N I X E L T X F L T B E B E N K E R H I
U S R X E E R C A S S A M W T D E R E H
T I X I E M P P R M F A M O U S R I D E
N L E N S E M F A B O C O T C O W R H D
Z V Y G O N K M T N Y U S Z K X A E C S
Y E D T R A T I I L X E S V H G S Z R U
X R Z N E J S N O P A E W R A L H L U N
M S Y O U S L B N M A N S S I S I A H D
M M V I O U A U O V A F D O I D N C C R
O I B T L T N N F W R B G T E H G R H E
P T X U U K B K I H U D I P S L T E T D
Q H N L T X B U N K E R H I L L O I R N
I S O O I P O E D M B I S E T H N T O E
V Y P V O M I N E M E N B O S T O N N R
X Z D E B Y E U P A U L R E V E R E B R
C O N R O D W K E R R E X D A U I A D U
N Z S A O B O N N D I X G N I N R A W S
Z R E R B C T O D B C N C A N D W A R N
F E E S O L N B E P A T C R I O W A N T
E U S T O H A O N D R U G E S T Y X O Y
Z O X E N I T N C Z W Y R O T C I V R Z
Y L E X V A L L E Y F O R G E O N M C X
L U L U L U L A M A N I C A P N N O H K
```

Bell, Boston, British, Bunker Hill, Concord, Declaration of Independence, Famous Ride, Land, Lantern, Lexington, Massacre, Midnight, Minutemen, North Church, Patriot, Paul Revere, Princeton, Revolution, Sea, Silversmith, Surrender, Tax, Tea, Tower, Valley Forge, Victory, War, Warning, Washington, Weapons

33

Tangle Table

Using the numbers 1-10, figure out which numbers should go across the top row and down the left side column. When a number from the top row is added with a number from the left side column, the sum will equal the number in the box where their rows meet. (See the example which has been done for you: 10 + 4 = 14.) Then complete the rest of the empty boxes. The totals must match the numbers already there.

+						4			
	6				10				
10		20			14				
		15		12					
			12						7
	18				13				
		18	16			10			
		13	10				9		
		10			5				
			13						
						4			

Puzzle by
Amanda Costa
Chelmsford, MA

● ● ● ● ● ● ● ● ● ● ● ● ● ● ● ● ● ● ●

There were two boys that looked exactly the same. They both had blonde hair and blue eyes, but they were not twins. Each was born to the same mother on the same day. Explain this.

Riddle by
Mindy Townsend
Aiken, SC

START

FINISH!

Maze by
Joseph Allyn
New Haven, MO

35

Boat Word Search

Shawn Patoka, Menasha, WI

```
A G U G R G H B O H Y D R O F O I L C A T A M A R A N
H O E D A M U U E A Y S A I L B O A T B E S E Y E R E
P O N T O O N S H O R E N H E L Z X Y A Y S E B A B E
C H O N Y Z E P H O R G O N D O L A N R E Y W X W E L
A A N A O N E E C H E I N S H E E N E G C H I E C E O
B B G O E E N E H E F O D A M E A M E E H E L P D A M
I E N H O P L D E M H E L P H O U S E B O A T L L E S
N N A O P E P B D T E M O T O H I L P O U I U I I P L
C E M H C A N O E P L E S I V I P O E U T N G O N D O
R M R H A T N A A T O K N E E P L O P T B O T N I I E
U O E E R M E T N H T O P E R R A P A B O S S E R Y E
I N H H R H F L A G H B T C C I C D E O A A B C E Z Q
S O S N I O C V A W A X D E R E V F R A R F D B E F G
E P I O E D K L U V T Y U H A U G H T R D P A X O Y P
R O F E R O W B O A T L D I F T T S A D R V A W Q C D
S O T M N E F G R S W X G F T F S O J C U H A T D R U
L L R E O K B G I F J G H Y R H O P Q R N R S Z E S R
H H O M P L E O I I I G M N S I C M N U A G A F B H M
O M P E N M P L E J R B R J A K V A C I B I J C K C L
O N S P O N O C K M N O L C U D I L Y S O J K D I D H
W E B B A T T L E S H I P O P N J H A E U L B Z E T I
E M O T O R Y A C H T D M N G O K P Q R T M N K G B A
```

pontoons	carrier	outboard cruiser	barge
speedboat	rowboat	sailboat	ferry
houseboat	canoe	sport fisherman	tug
cabin cruisers	hovercraft	motoryacht	junk
battleship	outboard	sloop	gondola
sub	runabout	catamaran	hydrofoi

Animal Time

Each of the answers to the 14 clues is the name of a well-known animal. When you finish, read down the shaded column of boxes to find the name of something else.

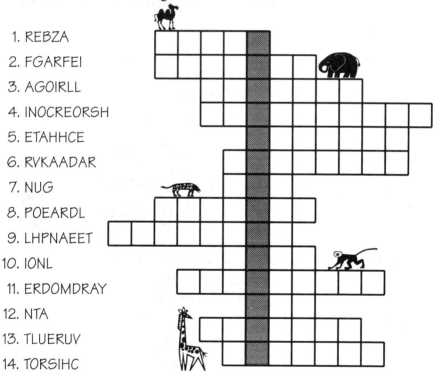

1. REBZA
2. FGARFEI
3. AGOIRLL
4. INOCREORSH
5. ETAHHCE
6. RVKAADAR
7. NUG
8. POEARDL
9. LHPNAEET
10. IONL
11. ERDOMDRAY
12. NTA
13. TLUERUV
14. TORSIHC

Puzzle by
Drew Magyar
Morrisville, PA

Where in the World?

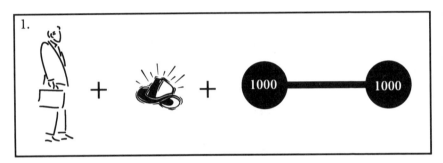

Jacob DeHart
Des Plaines, IL

Brian Ekstrom
Des Plaines, IL

Sarah Parkin
Des Plaines, IL

Backward and Forward

A palendrome is a word that is spelled the same backward as it is forward. Unscramble the palendromes in the word box and match each with a definition listed below.

1. Someone who takes care of you
2. A name for a lady
3. You get this kind of corn at a movie
4. Officials use this to find things
5. Lunch time
6. A Swedish rock group
7. A person who serves the church
8. A type of candy: Milk _____
9. A two year old

damma	ppo
tto	ardra
onon	unn
omm	baab
ddu	

Puzzle by
Jacqueline Giannelli
Yorktown Heights, NY

● ● ● ● ● ● ● ● ● ● ● ● ● ● ● ● ● ● ● ●

There was an old man from Peru,
Who was all tangled up in some glue.
He said, "Just as I feared,
I have glue in my beard,
Which is stuck to a toad and a shoe."

Michelle Shaw
Collinsville, IL

Presidents Crossword

Across

2. The only president who did not win an election to the office of the president
3. A child was born in the White House during this president's term
6. He was shot in Dallas, Texas
9. His picture is on the $20 bill
11. This was the first president of the United States
12. This was the first president to talk on the radio
13. The teddy bear was named after this president
14. "The buck stops here," was this man's famous saying
16. The president who took the Presidential Oath of Office while riding on an airplane
17. This man resigned as president
18. The 42nd president of the United States

Down

1. He was the leader of the Northern Army during the Civil War
4. The first president to live in the White House
5. Before being elected president, this man was a movie star
7. This president was shot at Ford's Theater
8. He had polio as a young man and was in a wheelchair
9. His picture is on the nickel
10. This man was a peanut farmer
14. This president had 15 children
15. His picture is on the $50 bill

Use FRoosevelt when referring to Franklin Roosevelt.
Use TRoosevelt when referring to Theodore Roosevelt.

Puzzle by
**Cynthia Villalobos
and Amanda Davis
Midland, TX**

States Word Search

Find the following state names in the puzzle. Words may be found up, down, sideways, backwards, and diagonally.

Alabama	Louisiana	Oklahoma
Alaska	Maine	Ohio
Arizona	Maryland	Oregon
Arkansas	Massachusetts	Rhode Island
California	Michigan	Pennsylvania
Colorado	Minnesota	South Carolina
Connecticut	Mississippi	South Dakota
Delaware	Missouri	Tennessee
Florida	Montana	Texas
Georgia	Nebraska	Utah
Hawaii	Nevada	Vermont
Idaho	New Hampshire	Virginia
Illinois	New Jersey	Washington
Indiana	New Mexico	West Virginia
Iowa	New York	Wisconsin
Kentucky	North Carolina	Wyoming
Kansas	North Dakota	

Word Search by
Robby Robinson
Menasha, WI

```
P E N N S Y L V A N I A H E A B C G K M I R U O S S I M H E
R O B I N A E L S O O L K B D E L A W A R E H R H M E I T F
N D T N A R A T R R P A A Z A Z W X A T D E A E E W K S K N
E T S A M S M N K T T B F B V K C Y S U V T R G F Y Z S P O
W K O O K O K C Y H W A O Y E T U K H H V U T O K O T I M R
M A N A C U F G H D I M A I N E H C I K S H M N S M U S A T
E T G E F T S Q T A R A S D Z M N K N E W Y O R K I V S K H
X A I K O H R U N K N P T A T W U V G C K O R K T N R I S C
I R T I A C Z Y O O F K O H U T U X T S A F G X Y G A P Y A
C V X W Z A N P R T L M T O M O H I O K R M D I Z O K P T R
O A A C Y R C K A A O A K A S O R E N E W J E R S E Y I E O
D I F D K O R W I S C O N S I N A E K N E W T R S A M P M L
I P I E Z L O U I S I A N A S S H Y A K I D S C I T V A I I
A M R W X I U T R H T K I N I C K K A N S A S R O N I T N N
D A P E R N Q H U E S H E K R P S O E T G S T E H X R S N A
C S R S K A R I Z O N A A H T A Z T A N N Y Z A T W G H E Z
T S X T A X H A K E F R T E R C D S C E T V T K Q O I A S L
K A R V G F O Y B H Z K V B D B F I O R I U A O B A N N O F
C C T I C O D H E M R A E C Z D E K R W F X C P X U I E T R
T H U R C C E Y Q Z S N Y U X S H E I O Q U A K Y I A N A O
K U X G V O I T K A O S H E B U A B K R L U L R Y O M I S M
O S U I K N S L I D T A X K Y C F T D E A F I T U R I K T E
D E I N U N L N L D C S O U T H D A K O T A F S Z Q C E V N
F T U I A E A E H I G F C D E A D T R K E R O K L A H O M A
R T Y A K C N W E N N O T R N H E W A B X T R D M N I R A D
T S K C O T D T S D S O P E N T R I D K A K N E N D G O R K
R U Z R T I R O D I E F I O E K O S D E S E I F D K A B Y A
O F B A S C K I T A K R R S S T G E O R G I A G A C N B L D
B O A O G U Y L I N E T D A S I R O Q X U I S H T O F Y A F
I R D C E T A O R A H C Z Y E R T C O L O R A D O O G Z N Q
M O N T A N A V E C F R E N E W H A M P S H I R E U M X D R
```

Chain Link

Each word in this series will begin with the last two letters of the word preceding it. For example, word two will begin with the letters "ce."

1. One time   once
2. The middle   _ _ _ _ _ _
3. To wear away   _ _ _ _ _
4. A piece of furniture   _ _ _ _
5. It covers your bones   _ _ _ _
6. An inner surface   _ _ _ _ _ _
7. This animal has antlers   _ _ _ _
8. When you rub the end of your pencil on paper   _ _ _ _ _
9. A plant grows from one of these   _ _ _ _
10. You go to school to get one of these   _ _ _ _ _ _ _ _ _
11. The beginning of something   _ _ _ _ _
12. Forever   _ _ _ _ _ _ _ _
13. A certain kind   _ _ _ _
14. All males and females   _ _ _ _ _ _
15. This person directs others   _ _ _ _ _ _
16. An age in history   _ _ _
17. You run this to win   _ _ _ _
18. One penny   _ _ _ _

Puzzle by
Russ Hoelzel
Menasha, WI

Joker's Code

Use the code to solve the puzzle.

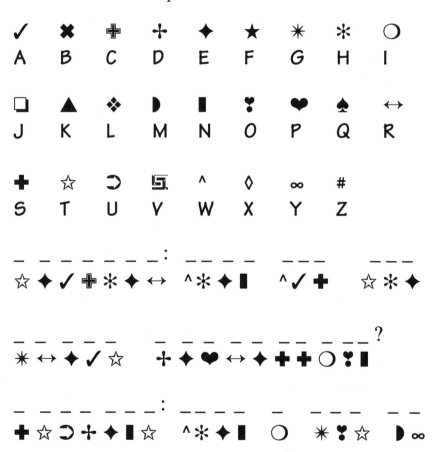

✓	✖	✚	✛	◆	★	✳	✱	○
A	B	C	D	E	F	G	H	I

▢	▲	❖	◗	▮	❣	♥	♠	↔
J	K	L	M	N	O	P	Q	R

✚	☆	⊃	卐	^	◊	∞	#
S	T	U	V	W	X	Y	Z

Puzzle by
Natalie Roszel
Tulsa, OK

Product Puzzle

Theresa Rusho, Syracuse, NY

Write the names of the products in the spaces, and unscramble the circled letters to find the name of the city where *Wheaties* cereal was first made: _ _ _ _ _ _ _ _ _ _ _

1. This flavored jelly-like dessert that "shakes" was first patented in 1845 as a gelatin dessert:

2. This transparent tape can be used instead of glue; 3M gave it the name in 1926:

3. This soda is one of the leading colas in America today; John S. Pemberton came up with the original formula in May, 1886:

4. This cleansing bar is 99 and 44/100 percent pure; it was invented in 1878 by the firm Proctor and Gamble:

5. This company that produces skin products (especially facial products) got its name originally because it "knocks exzema":

6. Robert Augustus Chesebrough invented this brand-name jelly product that can't be used on bread; however, it can be used as a burn ointment or to remove makeup:

Invention Search

Preparation of Materials:
1. Copy a list of the inventions and their point value for each player.
2. Prepare 10 sets of cut-out squares with letters of the alphabet on them. (10 complete alphabets)
   Example: [A] [B] [C]
3. Locate a timer, clock, or watch to indicate exactly three minutes.

Directions:
1. Dump all the letters in the center of the table.
2. Each player takes a list of the inventions.
3. Start the timer for three minutes.
4. Spell at least five of the inventions on the list, then spell other words with the remaining letters to earn bonus points.
5. Other words (with at least three letters) are worth one point per letter.
6. When the three minutes are up, total points. The player with the most points wins.

Airplane - 13	Frisbee - 12	Telephone - 14
Artificial Heart - 20	Hearing Aid - 15	Television - 15
Ax - 7	Plow - 9	Thermometer - 16
Back Scratcher - 18	Refrigerator - 18	Typewriter - 10
Bicycle - 12	Sewing Machine - 18	Velcro - 11
Can Opener - 9	Steamboat - 14	Zipper - 12

Game by
Jeni Ellis
Granbury, TX

Chain Link

Each word in this series will begin with the last two letters of the word preceding it. For example, word two will begin with the letters "on."

1. The bones of a body   skeleton
2. Something on a hamburger   _ _ _ _ _
3. By itself   _ _ _ _
4. A strong solution used to make soap   _ _ _
5. A bright color   _ _ _ _ _ _
6. One who owns   _ _ _ _ _
7. A period in time   _ _ _
8. A train drives on this   _ _ _ _ _ _ _ _
9. Opposite of subtraction   _ _ _ _ _ _ _ _
10. Beginning   _ _ _ _ _
11. Engrave a design   _ _ _ _
12. You sit on it   _ _ _ _ _
13. Gets wrinkles out of clothes   _ _ _ _
14. To a position on   _ _ _ _
15. Something in your mouth   _ _ _ _ _
16. The people spoken about   _ _ _ _
17. A country ruled by an emperor   _ _ _ _ _ _
18. To do over   _ _ _ _
19. A mixture of flour, milk, and fat   _ _ _ _ _
20. A flying white thing   _ _ _ _ _

Puzzle by
David Krueger
Menasha, WI

Pictures Worth A Thousand Words

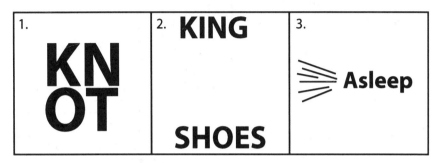

Puzzle by **Scott McKelvey, Midland, TX**

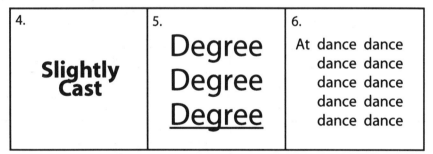

Puzzle by **Lindsey Rose, Midland, TX**

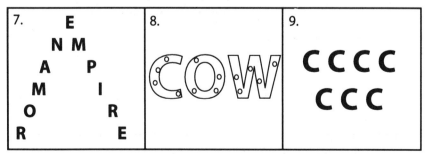

Puzzle by **Matthew Davis, Daniel Duarte, and Alex Del Giudice**
Stickney, IL

Dynamic Dolphins

1. The white-sided is not the male or the youngest dolphin.
2. The pink marked dolphin does not live in the Pacific Ocean, and neither does the cow.
3. The dolphin that is most common does not live in the Pacific or Atlantic Ocean.
4. The grown male dolphin does not live in the ocean that has six letters in its name, and its marking is not on the flank.
5. The Dall's is a "grand" old dolphin.
6. The cow sea mammal does have a yellow marking on it, and it does not live in the sea.

Dall's	white-sided	bottle-nosed	common	
				Atlantic Ocean
				Pacific Ocean
				Mediterranean Sea
				Arctic Ocean
				Grandmother
				Calf
				Bull
				Cow
				Yellow hourglass pattern
				Yellow banded flank
				White striped fin
				Pink belly

Puzzle by
Ashley Stringer
Gadsden, AL

7. The grandmother dolphin does live in the ocean and does not have a yellow marking on it.
8. The common dolphin does not have a pink or white marking on it, and it is not the baby.
9. The calf does not dwell in the ocean with eight letters in its spelling, and it does not have white markings.

Whale Scramble

Using the clues, find the name of one kind of whale. The letters are in certain places. Find them. For example, letter #1 will be S, R, H, or B.

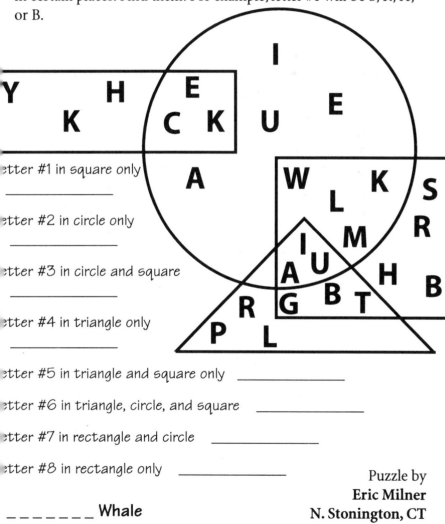

tter #1 in square only

_____

tter #2 in circle only

_____

tter #3 in circle and square

_____

tter #4 in triangle only

_____

tter #5 in triangle and square only   _____

tter #6 in triangle, circle, and square   _____

tter #7 in rectangle and circle   _____

tter #8 in rectangle only   _____

_ _ _ _ _ _ _ **Whale**

Puzzle by
Eric Milner
N. Stonington, CT

Rock and Mineral Word Search

```
A A I C C E R B B N T G C M U X M O X A D
I R V G M D A I G N E O U S A Q A K N B L
V I O W J D F T N D F L Z I A L T E D C K
R D O R D A A U I A K D R L M A Q C S I C
K E S U O Z E M P T C S F V Z U M R U L I
O C S B A U X I T E F L G E A Q W O K A H
Q K O E N R T N A Q A V N R E I W K W F P
L B I R S I B O N H L E T B L Y D K C O R
K A D Y E T L U I N B Z O U E A W K C O O
P S G L S E L S E D I M E N T A R Y S H M
S A E I E E L C Z A G A U N T G I E Q H A
N L Y V J I B O R N I T E X R N A E N N T
E T I H C A L A M W A O P E P E W L H I E
J N M D A K F L L F D R I L D G D T K S M
G E A R M X P F E B Q Q R A N T P S L Z E
```

Azurite   Breccia   Quartz
Basalt   Gold   Rock
Bauxite   Igneous   Sedimentary
Beryl   Malachite   Silver
Bituminous Coal   Metamorphic
Bornite   Mineral

Puzzle by
Stephanie Rice
Frankfort, KY

Mystery Word

My sixth letter is in lake, but not in snake.
My second letter is in break, but not in broke.
My seventh letter is in me, but not in my.
My fifth letter is in four, but not in fur.
My first letter is in take, but not in bake.
My fourth letter is in pour, but not in four.
My third letter is in dish, but not in fish.

What am I?

___ ___ ___ ___ ___ ___ ___
1   2   3   4   5   6   7

Puzzle by
Jeremy Grogg
Portland, IN

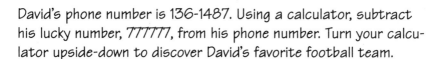

David's phone number is 136-1487. Using a calculator, subtract his lucky number, 777777, from his phone number. Turn your calculator upside-down to discover David's favorite football team.

Puzzle by
Tommy Mansell
Pottsville, PA

Hard at Work

Puzzle by **Jessica Dunn, Sugar Land, TX**

Four birds were building their nests. Each chose a different location for completing this task. The birds were preparing to lay eggs of different colors. After a full morning of hard work, they stopped to eat lunch. Using the clues, determine the location of each bird's nest, the color of its eggs, and the food it had for lunch. **Note:** two eggs are the same.

1. The blue jay did not build her nest in the shrub.
2. The mockingbird was not preparing to lay eggs with a plain white background color.
3. The house sparrow's nest location was not part of a tree.
4. The chickadee, who was not expecting blue eggs, was building her nest in either the hollow tree trunk or the eaves trough.
5. The blue jay never lays eggs with white backgrounds.
6. The fruit-eater has a nest in a shrub.
7. The mockingbird did not build her nest in the eaves trough, and she prefers nesting places close to the ground.
8. The bird that was building her nest in the eaves trough loves to eat some kind of seeds.
9. The blue jay is a daily customer at bird feeders.
10. The chickadee was one of the birds that was building a nest for white eggs.
11. The mockingbird's eggs will not have background colors of plain blue.
12. The tree branch, the hole in the trunk, and the eaves trough are quite high off the ground.

	Nest				Egg				Food			
	Shrub	Tree Branch	Hollow Trunk	Eaves Trough	Blue/White, Brown Spots	White, Red/Brown Spots	White, Red/Brown Spots	Blue, Brown Spots	Sunflower Seeds	Fruit	Insects	Seed on the Ground
Sparrow												
Chickadee												
Mockingbird												
Blue Jay												

● ●

Riddle Time

How can you make 30¢ with two coins if one of them is not a quarter?

Kristy Hudson
Newark, DE

The Dinner Party

Mr. Hunyjuckle is hosting a dinner party at his house. But, not all of his guests like each other. Help him figure out where everyone should sit.

1. Two men or two women cannot sit next to each other.
2. Mr. Hunyjuckle has a round table, but he won't be eating at the table.
3. Mr. Maltkins is in a fight with Ms. Jabber and Mr. Foster.
4. Mr. Foster is good friends with Ms. Jabber, who is on his left.
5. Mr. Winkler says Mr. Maltkins has bad breath.
6. Mrs. Alington and Mrs. O'Connor are in a fight.
7. Mrs. O'Connor wants to sit by Mr. Foster and Mr. Maltkins.
8. Mr. Foster is in chair #1.

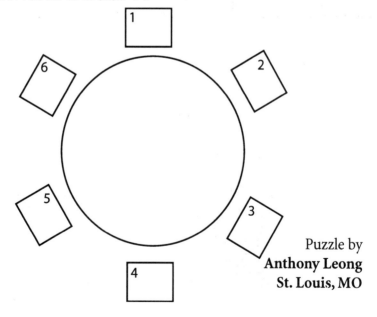

Puzzle by
**Anthony Leong
St. Louis, MO**

Circus Day

There were four children at the circus. Each child liked a different animal and a different kind of treat. Use the clues to figure them out.

1. A girl likes snow cones.
2. Mark said that he liked an animal that roared.
3. Mia likes popcorn.
4. The girl that likes snow cones likes horses.
5. Matt loves tigers.
6. Mark says that cotton candy is yucky.

	Soda	Popcorn	Snow Cone	Cotton Candy	Horse	Tiger	Lion	Elephant
Mary								
Mark								
Mia								
Matt								

Puzzle by
Carolyn Perez
Ft. Worth, TX

A Puzzle of the States

Use the clues to figure out who lives in each state.

1. Hilda lives in the state that is just south of Dorothy and Toto's home town.
2. Whitley is a potato farmer.
3. Wilma enjoys living on the east coast.
4. It is a shorter distance from Winnifred's home to the nation's capital than from Wilma's home.
5. Whitley ships 1,000 pounds of potatoes across the state line to Harry annually.
6. Wilber's state borders Willemina's state.
7. Winifred's son, Waldo, moved west to a state where he hopes to become successful in the corn business.
8. Hester and her family recently moved. Now Hester plans to visit Disney World everyday.
9. Herman is going to visit his brother, Herbert. First Herman will go to an airport in Charleston. About 10 hours later, his plane will land in Herbert's state.
10. Hugh feeds his dogsled team every night to prepare them for the Iditarod.
11. Hank lives just east of Hilda.
12. Willemina has lived in Augusta all her life.

Puzzle by
Frank Warpeha
Oak Brook, IL

	NH	OK	FL	WV	ID	IA	DE	CT	AK	ME	OR	HI	AR
Hilda													
Waldo													
Hank													
Willemina													
Hester													
Whitley													
Herman													
Winifred													
Harry													
Wilber													
Hugh													
Wilma													
Herbert													

Chain Link

Each word in this series will begin with the last two letters of the word preceding it. For example, word two will begin with the letters "om."

1. A part of a house   room
2. Beaten and cooked eggs   _ _ _ _ _
3. It puts you to sleep   _ _ _ _ _
4. What you do when you make a mistake   _ _ _ _ _
5. Octopuses live here   _ _ _
6. Some people search for eggs on this day   _ _ _ _ _ _
7. A volcano has an _____   _ _ _ _ _ _ _ _
8. More than zero, less than two   _ _ _
9. You sew with a _____   _ _ _ _ _ _
10. You hop with this   _ _ _
11. The outside of an egg   _ _ _ _ _ _ _
12. A large animal from South America   _ _ _ _ _
13. A horse is a _____   _ _ _ _ _ _
14. A reptile   _ _ _ _ _ _ _ _ _
15. You can peel an _____   _ _ _ _ _ _

Puzzle by
Samantha Luther
Menasha, WI

Complimentary Words Word Search

Marie Hause, Clearwater, FL

```
B U T H S B V E N H L L A N D E B E S B M
E U O V W M I E N L N A O I Y E B A R E Y
S B V I T M G A C V T H O I L V I R A I N
T V P H Y A M R V A M H O I U P L R N R R
C E T R A M K C E G E T R B S R M F E R V
B L A S W F U P G A R B E A S F U R E M U
I L W V I E B T U N T M B V U M B U X V N
M A S E N S I J L G B H J M P D E W C A B
I I H R N U O N R N E K E M U I L R I N E
M C N Y I P R E S N S E P P I P I E T V L
E E S G N E P U N O T P L S N R E P I L I
N P O O G U P M U U O I C N O E V U N V E
O S W O S F K J C I F I R R E T A D G M V
R E H D I K R N S T A V W M O T B R B S A
E B E C O N I T I I L M N O L Y L E S T B
B M H O P O M N Z C L O F R W S U P C M L
M L J P O P G L D O E R U P B U T U S U E
U V M O P F G L E E H R U P U T B S U E B
N C M P R M V E N H L U F I T U A E B N U
```

Best	Special	Nice	Beautiful
Great	Winning	Good	Pretty
Uplifting	Exciting	Unbelievable	Wow
Fun	Best of All	Number One	Super Duper
Super	Terrific	Kind	Very Good

Brain Twisters!

Sports Scramble

Nicky, Emily, Mark, Ashley, Becky, and Sam are really involved in their favorite sports. In fact, they've gotten so caught up in the action that the letters of their names have gotten mixed with the letters in the names of their favorite sports. Can you sort out who likes what?

1. EKSYHLHCYOEA

   person _____

   sport _____

2. NRKISNEAMT

   person _____

   sport _____

3. MBLASSABLEA

   person _____

   sport _____

4. OLIYBTOFELAML

   person _____

   sport _____

5. OTCDAEBBINKYMN

   person _____

   sport _____

6. ROICNYSCKEC

   person _____

   sport _____

Puzzle by
Virginia Hoover
Olive Branch, MS

Candy Kitchen

See if you can unmix this sticky mess by identifying each person's last name and the candy she is making.

1. Miss Kent had peanuts in her hair.
2. Angie did not make peanut brittle.
3. Amy had lollipop mix in her hair.
4. Miss Mayln made lollipops.
5. Alecia's initials are A.K.
6. Angie baked chocolate.
7. A.S. made candy bars.
8. Angie's initials are A.T.

	Thomas	Kent	Smith	Mayln	Fudge	Peanut Brittle	Candy Bars	Lollipops
Amy								
Angie								
Annie								
Alecia								

Puzzle by
Ashley Gazi
Belle Vernon, PA

Where's Charlotte?

Charlotte got lost at the mall. Help her mother find here. While you are looking for Charlotte, how many of these other things can you find?

lovebirds
doll
train
four Easter eggs
American flag
boom box
two plants
escaped convict

Puzzle by
Mandy Webb
Monticello, KY

Answers

to

Puzzles

Solar System Word Search, Page 7

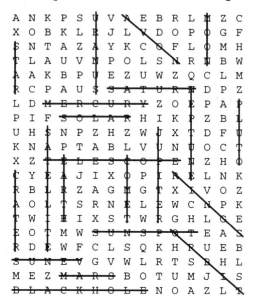

```
A N K P S U V A E B R L M Z C
X O B K L R J L V D O P O G F
S N T A Z A Y K C O F L O M H
T L A U V N P O L S N R N B W
A A K B P U E Z U W Z Q C L M
R C P A U S S A T U R N D P Z
L D M E R C U R Y Z O E P A P
P I F S O L A R H I K P Z B L
U H S N P Z H Z W U X T D F U
K N A P T A B L V U N U O C T
X Z T L E S C O P E N Z H O
C Y E A J I X O P I R E L N K
R B L R Z A G M G T X L V O Z
A O L T S R N E L E W C N P K
T W I H I X S T W R G H L C E
E O T M W S U N S P O T E A S
R D E W F C L S Q K H R U E B
S U N E V G V W L R T S R H L
M E Z M A R S B O T U M J I S
B L A C K H O L E N O A Z L R
```

Spacey Crossword, Page 9

<u>Across</u>
2. space
5. Pluto
6. Neptune
9. Mars
11. galaxies
12. comet
14. stars
15. Mercury
17. Uranus

<u>Down</u>
1. cosmonaut
3. explore
4. Saturn
7. Earth
8. extraterrestrial
10. black hole
13. astronaut
16. rocket

Trans: blank

Astronauts Landing, Page 10

Gagarin, April 1961, Vostok I, First in space
Shepard, May 1961, Freedom VII, First American in space
Armstrong, July 1961, Apollo 2, First to land on the moon
Tereshkova, June 1963, Vostok 6, First woman in space
Glenn, February 1962, Friendship 7, First American in orbit

Outer Space Crossword, Page11

Across
4. sun
5. Saturn
6. spiral
7. Venus
11. Neptune
14. Solar System
15. Earth
16. meteorite

Down
1. Asteriod Belt
2. Mars
3. Jupiter
8. Uranus
9. Mercury
10. star
12. meteor
13. Pluto

Confused Cats, Page 12

Sally Smith, Dopey, Orange
Ann Brown, Skittles, Black
Sue Silver, Pumpkin, Gray

Picture Graph, Page 13

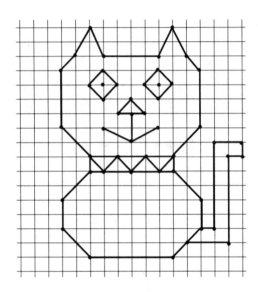

Hobbies Word Scramble, Page 14

1. painting
2. dancing
3. horseback riding
4. piano
5. sports
6. music
7. cheerleading
8. fishing

9. camping
10. karate
11. swimming
12. drawing
13. rollerblading
14. ice skating
15. skiing

Scrambled Phrases, Page 15

1. Trust me.
2. Look before you leap.
3. A penny saved is a penny earned.
4. The early bird gets the worm.
5. No pain, no gain.
6. See a penny, pick it up and all the day you will have good luck.
7. When it rains it pours.
8. April showers bring May flowers.
9. It is always darkest before the dawn.

1. Skating on thin ice
2. Don't count your chickens before they hatch.
3. Where there's a will there's a way.
4. An apple a day keeps the dentist away.
5. Fighting like cats and dogs
6. Too many cooks spoil the broth.
7. Feed a cold, starve a fever.

Lunch at School, Page 16

1. Jessica, Math, Dr Pepper
2. Kim, Science, Diet Coke
3. Kathy, Health, Milk
4. Danielle, English, Orange Juice
5. Rachel, History, Apple Juice

Lunch Bunch, Page 17

Andy: pizza, Coke, blizzard
Elizabeth: chicken, milk, candy bar
Joe: salad, water, no dessert
Mr. Lowe: steak, Pepsi, ice cream
Mary: hamburger, orange pop, milk shake
Hank: eggs, soda, banana split

Desk Arrangements, Page 18

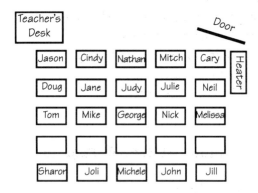

Can You Find Your Way? Page 19

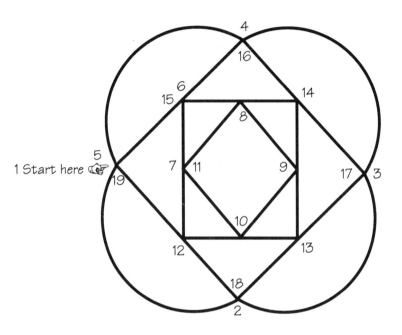

This is only one suggestion. There are several ways to solve this puzzle.

The Shopping Spree, Page 20

Kevin: black shirt
George: blue pants
Mike: yellow hat
Harry: red sneakers
Chadd: green jacket
Chris: brown socks

Brain Twisters!

Fruit and Vegetable Stand Mix-up, Page 21

1. carrots; 2. apples; 3. green beans; 4. peaches; 5. peas; 6. pears;
7. broccoli; 8. pecans; 9. tomatoes; 10. cauliflower

Mystery Word Puzzle, Page 24

Alligator

Riddle, Page 24

a needle and thread

Jumble, Page 25

Same   Latest
Biology   Official
America

A Little Lamb

Magnificent Mathematicians

Regiomontanus: Germany, 1533, Trigonometry
John Napier: Scotland, 1614, Logarithms
Euclid: Greece, 300 B.C., Geometry
Sir Isaac Newton: Britain, 1687, Calculus

Picture Graph, Page 28

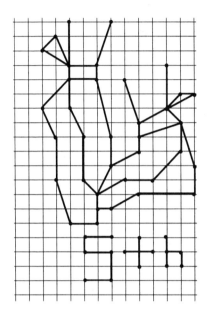

Riddle, Page 29

A horseshoe

A Mixed-Up Car Race, Page 30

Bill: yellow, 6th place
Rob: orange, 5th place
Zack: red, 2nd place
Adam: blue, 3rd place

Chad: green, 4th place
Peter: black, 7th place
Matt: white, 1st place

Brain Twisters!

Horse Race, Page 31

Kate: Magic, Jennie, 2nd place; Jim: Lightning, Laura, 4th place; Jessie: Eclipse, Becky, 1st place; Ceri: Princess, Emily, 3rd place

French Explorers, Page 32

Samuel: de Champlain, Canada, 1608; Robert: La Salle, Gulf of Mexico, 1682; Jacques: Cartier, St. Lawrence, 1534; Louis: Joliet, Mississippi River, 1673

Early Revolutionary Days, Page 33

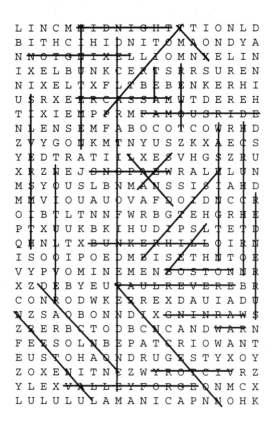

Tangle Table, Page 34

+	3	9	10	6	8	7	4	2	5	1
3	6					10				
10			20				**14**			
5			15			12				
6				12						7
9		18				13				
8			18		16			10		
4		13		10					9	
1		10					5			
7				13						
2								4		

Riddle, Page 34

The boys were triplets.

Maze, Page 35

Boat Word Search, Page 36

```
A G U G R G H B O H Y D R O F O I L C A T A M A R A N
H O E D A M U U E A Y S A I L B O A T B E S E Y E R E
P O N T O O N S H O R E N H E L Z X Y A Y S E B A B E
C H O N Y Z E P H O R G O N D O L A N R E Y W X W E L
A A N A O N E E C H E I N S H E E N E G C H I E C E O
B B G O E E N E H E F O D A M E A M E E H E L P D A M
I E N H O P L D E M H E L P H O U S E B O A T L L E S
N N A O P E P B D T E M O T O H I L P O U I U I I P L
C E M H C A N U E P L E S I V I P O E U T N G O N D O
R M R H A T N A A T O K N E E P L O P T B O T N I I E
U O E E R M E T N H T O P E R R A P A B O S S E R Y E
I N H H R H F L A G H B T C C I C D E O A A B C E Z Q
S O S N I O C V A W A X D E R E V F R A R F D B E F G
E P I O E D K L U V T Y U H A U G H T R D P A X O Y P
R O F E R O W B O A T L D I F T T S A D R V A W Q C D
S O T M N E F G R S W X G F T F S O J C U H A T D R U
L L R E O K B G I F J G H Y R H O P Q R N R S Z E S R
H H O M P L E O I I I G M N S I C M N U A G A F B H M
O M P E N M P L E J R B R V A K V A C I B I J C K C L
O N S P O N O C K M N O L C U D I L Y S O J K D I D H
W E B B A T T L E S H I P O P N J H A E U L B Z E T I
E M O T O R Y A C H T D M N G O X P Q R T M N K G B A
```

Animal Time, Page 37

1. zebra; 2. giraffe; 3. gorilla; 4. rhinoceros; 5. cheetah; 6. aardvark; 7. gnu; 8. leopard; 9. elephant; 10. lion; 11. dromedary; 12. ant; 13. vulture; 14. ostrich

African Animals

Where in the World? Page 38

1. Manhatton
2. Minneapolis
3. Seattle

Backward and Forward, Page 39

1. mom
2. madam
3. pop
4. radar
5. noon

6. abba
7. nun
8. dud
9. tot

President's Crossword, Page 41

Across
2. Ford
3. Cleveland
6. Kennedy
9. Jackson
11. Washington
12. Wilson
13. TRoosevelt
14. Truman
16. Johnson
17. Nixon
18. Clinton

Down
1. Grant
4. Adams
5. Reagan
7. Lincoln
8. FRoosevelt
9. Jefferson
10. Carter
14. Tyler
15. Madison

States Word Search, Page 42

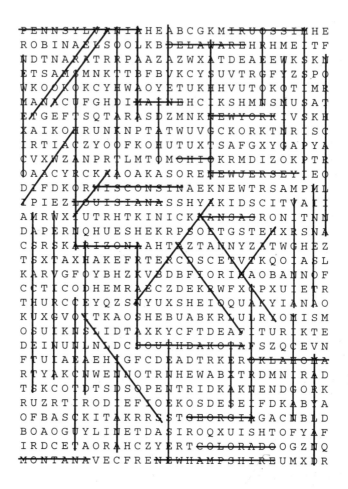

```
PENNSYLVANIAHEABCGKMIRUOSSIMHE
ROBINAELSOOLKBDELAWAREHRHMEITF
NDTNARXTRRPAAZAZWXATDEALEWKSKN
ETSAMSMNKTTBFBVKCYSUVTRGFYZSPO
WKOOROKCYHWAOYETUKHHVUTOKOTIMR
MANACUFGHDIMAINEHCIKSHMNSMUSAT
ELGEFTSQTARASDZMNKNEWYORKIVSKH
XAIKOHRUNKNPTATWUVGCKORKTNRISC
IRTIACZYOOFKOHUTUXTSAFGXYGAPYA
CVXWZANPRTLMTOMOHIOKRMDIZOKPTR
OAACYRCKXAOAKASORENEWJERSEYIEO
DIFDKORWISCONSINAEKNEWTRSAMPML
ZPIEZLOUISIANASSHYXKIDSCITVAII
AMRWXTUTRHTKINICKKANSASRONITNN
DAPERNQHUESHEKRPSOETGSTEMXRSNA
CSRSKARIZONAAHTXZTANNYZATWGHEZ
TSXTAXHAKEFRTERCDSCEIVTKQOIASL
KARVGFOYBHZKVBDBFIORIXAOBANNOF
CCTICODHEMRAECZDEKRWFXCPXUIETR
THURCCEYQZSNYUXSHEIQQUAKYIANAO
KUXGVOXTKAOSHEBUABKRLULRXOMISM
OSUIKNSLIDTAXKYCFTDEAFITURIKTE
DEINUNLNLDCSOUTHDAKOTAFSZQCEVN
FTUIALAEHIGFCDEADTRKEROKLAHOMA
RTYAKCNWENNOTRNHEWABXTRDMNIRAD
TSKCOTDTSDSOPENTRIDKAKNENDGORK
RUZRTIRODIEFIOEKOSDESEIFDKABYA
OFBASCKITAKRRSSTGEORGIAGACNBLD
BOAOGUYLINETDASIROQXUISHTOFYAF
IRDCETAORAHCZYERTCOLORADOOGZNQ
MONTANAVECFRENEWHAMPSHIREUMXDR
```

Chain Link, Page 44

1. once; 2. center; 3. erode; 4. desk; 5. skin; 6. inside; 7. deer; 8. erase; 9. seed; 10. education; 11. onset; 12. eternity; 13. type; 14. people; 15. leader; 16. era; 17. race; 18. cent

Joker's Code, Page 45

Teacher: When was the Great Depression? Student: When I got my report card.

Product Puzzle, Page 46

1. Jell-O
2. Scotch Tape
3. Coca-Cola
4. Ivory Soap
5. Noxzema
6. Vaseline

Minneapolis

Chain Link, Page 48

1. skeleton; 2. onion; 3. only; 4. lye; 5. yellow; 6. owner; 7. era; 8. railroad; 9. addition; 10. onset; 11. etch; 12. chair; 13. iron; 14. onto; 15. tooth; 16. them; 17. empire; 18. redo; 19. dough; 20. ghost

Pictures Worth A Thousand Words, Page 49

1. square knot; 2. hiking shoes; 3. fast asleep; 4. slightly overcast;
5. third degree; 6. attendance; 7. the rise and fall of the Roman
Empire; 8. holy cow; 9. Seven Seas

Dynamic Dolphins, Page 50

Common: Mediterranean Sea, bull, yellow hourglass pattern
Bottle-nosed: Arctic Ocean, calf, pink belly
White-sided: Atlantic Ocean, cow, yellow banded flank
Dall's: Pacific Ocean, grandmother, white striped fin

Whale Scramble, Page 51

Humpback Whale

Rock and Mineral Word Search, Page 52

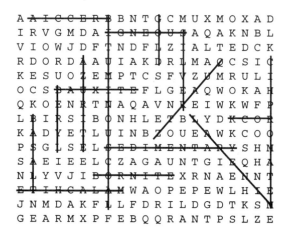

Mystery Word, Page 53

Tadpole

Number Puzzle, Page 53

Oilers

Hard at Work, Page 55

Sparrow: eaves trough, white with red/brown spots, seed on ground
Chickadee: hollow trunk, white with red/brown spots, insects
Mockingbird: shrub, blue/white with brown spots, fruit
Blue Jay: tree branch, blue and brown spots, sunflower seeds

Riddle, Page 55

One of the coins is a nickel, the **other one** is a quarter.

The Dinner Party, Page 56

1. Mr. Foster; 2. Ms. Jabber; 3. Mr. Winkler; 4. Mrs. Alington; 5. Mr. Maltkins; 6. Mrs. O'Connor

Circus Day, Page 57

Mary: snow cone, horse
Mark: soda, lion
Mia: popcorn, elephant
Matt: cotton candy, tiger

A Puzzle of the States, Page 59

Hilda, Oklahoma; Waldo, Iowa; Hank, Arkansas; Willemina, Maine; Hester, Florida; Whitley, Idaho; Herman, West Virginia; Winifred, Deleware; Harry, Oregon; Wilber, New Hampshire; Hugh, Alaska; Wilma, Connecticut; Herbert, Hawaii

Chain Link, Page 60

1. room; 2. omlet; 3. ether; 4. erase; 5. sea; 6. easter; 7. eruption; 8. one; 9. needle; 10. leg; 11. eggshell; 12. llama; 13. mammal; 14. alligator; 15. orange

Complimentary Words Word Search, Page 61

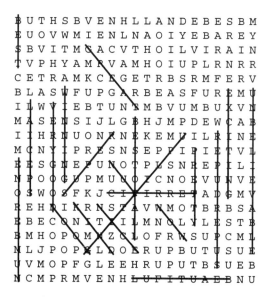

Sports Scramble, Page 62

1. Ashley, hockey; 2. Mark, tennis; 3. Sam, baseball; 4. Emily, football; 5. Becky, badminton; 6. Nicky, soccer

Candy Kitchen, Page 63

Amy: Mayln, lollipops
Angie: Thomas, fudge
Annie: Smith, candy bars
Alecia: Kent, peanut brittle

Where's Charlotte, Page 65

Shop 'Til You Drop Game Cards

Cut the cards out to use with the board game on page 23.

Parties 'N Such Used $1 to buy a kazoo. Lose 1 point	**Parties 'N Such** Spent $3 on a gadget that didn't work. Lose 2 points	**Parties 'N Such** Used brother's allowance on yourself. Lose 3 points
Parties 'N Such Bought candy for your sister's party. Earn 2 points	**Parties 'N Such** Threw a surprise party for a friend. Earn 3 points.	**Parties 'N Such** Bought your friend a birthday present. Earn 1 point.
Toyland Catch a person stealing. Earn 3 points.	**Toyland** Buy a gift with your own money. Earn 2 points.	**Toyland** Buy yourself a toy in front of your brother. Lose 2 points.
Toyland Security caught you shoplifting. Lose 3 points.	**Toyland** Knocked down the stuffed animals. Lose 1 point.	**Toyland** Buy your sister her favorite toy. Earn 1 point.
Quincy's Clothes Buy your sister a prom dress. Earn 2 points.	**Quincy's Clothes** Help your grandma pay for an outfit. Earn 3 points.	**Quincy's Clothes** Waste mom's money on a pair of shoes. Lose 2 points.

Quincy's Clothes Spend $5 on a key ring for yourself. Lose 1 point.	**Quincy's Clothes** Buy your dad a tie for Father's Day. Earn 1 point.	**Quincy's Clothes** Spend $100 on "show-off" clothes. Lose 3 points.
Pierre's Pizza Buy a lemonaid for a friend. Earn 1 point.	**Pierre's Pizza** Get into a food fight with the manager. Lose 3 points.	**Pierre's Pizza** Buy a whole pizza all for yourself. Lose 2 points.
Pierre's Pizza Buy your friend her favorite pizza. Earn 3 points.	**Pierre's Pizza** Win "customer of the day" trophy. Earn 2 points.	**Pierre's Pizza** Drop your pizza on the ground. Lose 1 point.
Esprit Shop Fake sick so you don't have to shop. Lose 2 points.	**Esprit Shop** Take your brother shopping for an outfit. Earn 3 points.	**Esprit Shop** Buy a stuffed animal for a friend. Earn 2 points.
Esprit Shop Spend your lunch money on ice cream. Lose 1 point.	**Esprit Shop** Buy markers for your school project. Earn 1 point.	**Esprit Shop** Spend $6 to see a movie you don't like. Lose 3 points.
Penny's Place Buy decorations for Grandma. Earn 1 point	**Penny's Place** Buy Christmas gifts for your family. Earn 3 points.	**Penny's Place** Miss your aunt's party to go shopping. Lose 1 point.

Penny's Place	Penny's Place	Penny's Place
Buy dad fishing supplies. Earn 2 points.	Skip school to go shopping. Lose 3 points.	Spend $5 playing video games. Lose 2 points.